The Ultimate Guide to Social Media for Event Planners

Table of Contents

1. Introduction 2
2. Unveiling the Power of Social Media 3
    2.1. Connecting Far and Wide 3
    2.2. Dynamic Real-Time Interaction 3
    2.3. Platforms for Promotion and Branding 4
    2.4. Measuring Impact and Reach 4
    2.5. Building a Community 4
3. Choosing your Ideal Social Media Platforms 6
    3.1. Identifying Your Target Audience 6
    3.2. Reflecting Your Brand Personality 6
    3.3. Evaluating The Nature of Your Events 7
    3.4. Determining Your Marketing Objectives 7
    3.5. Resource Allocation 8
    3.6. Benchmarking and Competition Evaluation . . . 8
4. Creating a Winning Social Media Strategy 9
    4.1. Understanding Your Objectives 9
    4.2. Identifying Your Audience 9
    4.3. Choosing the Right Social Media Platform(s) . . . 10
    4.4. Developing Your Brand's Voice and Tone 10
    4.5. Constructing a Content Calendar 11
    4.6. Utilizing Social Media Advertising 11
    4.7. Tracking, Analyzing, and Adapting 11
5. Mastering Event Promotion on Social Media 13
    5.1. Understanding Your Audience 13
    5.2. Creating a Social Media Calendar 13
    5.3. Designing Engaging Social Media Graphics 14
    5.4. Leveraging the Power of Hashtags 14
    5.5. Using Paid Advertisements 15

5.6. Collaborating With Influencers 15

5.7. Post-Event Social Media Activity 15

6. Crafting Engaging Content that Rallies Audience 17

6.1. Understanding Your Audience 17

6.2. Tailoring Content According to Platform 18

6.3. Implementing Variety and Creativity 18

6.4. Focusing on Quality 18

6.5. Incorporating Interactive Elements 19

6.6. Telling a Story 19

6.7. Using Clear Call-to-Actions 19

6.8. Experiment and Measure 20

7. Best Practices for Audience Interaction 21

7.1. Strategize Your Audience Interaction 21

7.2. Creating a Social Media Calendar 22

7.3. Personalizing Your Audience Interaction 22

7.4. Employing Varied Content Formats 23

7.5. Responding to Audience 23

8. Leveraging Social Media for Event-Day Engagement 25

8.1. The Power of Live-Tweeting and Instagram Stories 25

8.2. Facebook Live And Its Influence 26

8.3. Harnessing LinkedIn for Professional Events 26

8.4. Snapchat Geofilters: The Fun Element 27

8.5. Post-Event Interactions: The Icing On The Cake 27

9. Post-Event Debriefing in the Digital Age 28

9.1. The Concept of Digital Debriefing 28

9.2. The Importance of Post-Event Debriefing in the Digital Age . . 28

9.3. Dissecting Your Social Media Metrics 29

9.4. Comprehending Audience Feedback 29

9.5. Utilizing Feedback for Future Improvements 30

9.6. Staying Connected Post-Event 30

10. Measuring Your Social Media Impact 32

    10.1. Understanding Social Media Metrics 32

    10.2. The Importance of Social Media Analytics 32

    10.3. Analyzing Engagement Metrics 33

    10.4. Tracking Reach and Impressions 33

    10.5. Evaluating The Click-Through Rate (CTR) 33

    10.6. Monitoring Follower Growth 34

    10.7. Measuring Conversions 34

    10.8. Social Media Listening 34

    10.9. Taking Stock of your Competitors 34

    10.10. Utilizing Social Media Audit 34

11. Staying Ahead: Anticipating Social Media Trends 36

    11.1. Identifying Emerging Trends 36

    11.2. Implementing Predictive Analytics 36

    11.3. Cultivating a Culture of Experimentation and Quick
Adoption 37

    11.4. Utilizing Influencers' Insights 37

    11.5. Incorporating Feedback and Hosting Interactive Sessions . . 38

    11.6. Observing Competitive Landscape 38

Marketing is no longer about the stuff that you make, but about the stories you tell.

— Seth Godin

Chapter 1. Introduction

Welcome to your one-way ticket to ruling the social media world, dear Event Planners! Prepare to delve into this special report, The Ultimate Guide to Social Media for Event Planners - a vibrant hub of groundbreaking strategies, genius trends, innovative tricks and time-tested techniques. If you are passionate about executing flawless events and wish to magnify your influence in the digital world, then buckle up! This guide will shine light upon the landscape of various social media platforms, teach you how to create engaging content, and enlighten you with the best practices for audience interaction and event promotion. Experience the joy of leveling up your craft and transforming your events into trendsetters, just by turning the pages. This report is your secret ingredient to become a social media maestro, so, come on, let's boost your career to the sky!

Chapter 2. Unveiling the Power of Social Media

Welcome, illustrious event planners, to an extraordinary journey of discovery. Here, we peel back the layers of misunderstanding and misconception to truly uncover the power vested in social media. Understand that at its core, social media is not just about sharing memes, posting vacation pictures or catching up on news. It is, in fact, a vibrant, dynamic and sometimes overwhelming space for interaction, engagement and influence.

2.1. Connecting Far and Wide

To begin with, one of the primary allures of social media lies in its boundless connectivity. Born from the digital age, social media platforms eradicate barriers of geography, breaking territorial confines to reach potentially billions of users worldwide. For event planners, this means that you have an immediate, far-reaching communication channel to distribute information, engage with attendees, and build hype around your event. Harnessing social media effectively can make your event resonate on a global spectrum in just a few clicks.

2.2. Dynamic Real-Time Interaction

What amplifies the power of these connections is the capability to engage in real-time. Announcements are immediate, responses are spontaneous, and problem-solving occurs almost instinctively. This immediacy, bolstered by the underlying interactivity of social media, fosters a sense of closeness between event planners and their audience. People not only become audience members for the event, but they can also have a say, provide feedback, and partake in real-time event-related discussions. The opportunity to strengthen ties with attendees, build anticipation, and shape event experiences as per real-time feedback immensely adds to the power of social media.

2.3. Platforms for Promotion and Branding

Social media further serves as an impactful promotion and branding platform. The visual aesthetics, striking graphics, and compelling narratives of social media content can immensely fuel the excitement for any event. By creating a unique digital brand around your event, you not only establish a distinct identity, but you also stand out from the crowd. Social networks like Instagram, Facebook, Twitter, and LinkedIn, each with their unique nuances, help in crafting an engaging and visually appealing digital persona for your event.

2.4. Measuring Impact and Reach

The power of social media extends to its built-in ability to measure the impact, delve deep into analytics, and gauge the effectiveness of various initiatives. This becomes invaluable for event planners, who can gain insights into attendance trends, popular content, and overall audience reception. Effective evaluation metrics like the number of likes, shares, comments, or even the sentiment behind comments can be utilized to modulate and maneuver your event planning strategies accordingly.

2.5. Building a Community

Finally, social media provides an avenue to form strong, interactive communities. Whether through groups on Facebook, hashtags on Twitter, or even event pages on LinkedIn, the digital space has the potential to foster robust, engaged communities who resonate with your event's essence. Cultivating such a dedicated community far surpasses the benefits of one-time interactions as it encourages loyalty, promotes recurring participation, and builds a reputable brand legacy.

In conclusion, it's clear that social media's power extends far beyond what meets the eye. Its extensive reach, real-time interaction capabilities, promotion and branding potential, and ability to measure impact, make it a potent tool in an event planner's arsenal. As we peel back the layers of each social media platform, we can engage with its intrinsic strengths and qualities, and in the chapters to follow, we will do precisely that. Learn how to adapt, maneuver and harness the sprawling landscape of social media, making your event a resounding digital success story. Let's dive further into this fascinating voyage!

Chapter 3. Choosing your Ideal Social Media Platforms

In the sprawling digital landscape, choosing the right social media platforms to focus your event planning efforts on can mean the difference between a grand success and a dismal performance. This chapter is dedicated to helping you evaluate and select the ideal social media platforms that resonate with your target audience, the nature of your events, and the goals you wish to achieve.

3.1. Identifying Your Target Audience

Successful social media marketing for event planning often begins with a clear understanding of who your audience is. Exploring the demographics, interests, and online behaviours of your intended audience can provide crucial insights into the social media platforms they are most active on.

Usually, younger audiences may be more active on platforms like Instagram or Snapchat, while a slightly older crowd may be found on Facebook or LinkedIn. Understanding where your audience spends their time is the first step in knowing which platforms to prioritize.

Use various tools like Facebook Insights, Instagram Insights or Google's Demographics and Interests Reports to get an in-depth analysis of your target audience.

3.2. Reflecting Your Brand Personality

Each social media platform has its unique flavour, audience, and style of content. While Facebook is traditionally associated with connection and community, Instagram is image-centric, focusing more on aesthetics and storytelling. LinkedIn is the hub for professional networking and industry-focused content, whereas Twitter is ideal for sharing thoughts real-time and starting discussions on trending topics.

Your choice of platform should be a reflection of your brand personality. If your events are formal, industry-specific conferences, Linkedin might be a better choice. If you're organizing an art festival or a fashion show, visually-driven platforms like Instagram or Pinterest would work best.

3.3. Evaluating The Nature of Your Events

The types of events you plan and execute also have a direct bearing on the choice of your platforms. Festivals, concerts, or similar large-scale public events often perform well on Facebook with its event-specific features allowing to create event pages, invite people, and even sell tickets. Professional seminars, webinars, and industry conferences may gain more traction on LinkedIn, where relevant professionals are more likely to engage with the content.

3.4. Determining Your Marketing Objectives

What are your key goals from social media marketing? Are you looking to create awareness, generate event sign-ups, or build a community? Answering these questions can guide your platform choice as each platform offers different advantages.

Facebook's vast user base and comprehensive functionality make it ideal for reaching a broad audience and creating community engagement. In contrast, Twitter's real-time communication feature is excellent for instant updates and real-time interactions. Instagram, with its visual-centric approach, is great for showcasing event highlights, creating a buzz, and indirectly pushing sign-ups through captivating imagery.

3.5. Resource Allocation

In the end, resource allocation also plays a crucial role in platform selection. Each platform demands time for creating content, engaging with audience, and monitoring performance. Evaluate how your available resources align with the needs of your chosen platforms. If you lack a dedicated graphic design support, a text-heavy platform like Twitter or LinkedIn may suit you best.

3.6. Benchmarking and Competition Evaluation

Lastly, consider taking a cue from your successful competitors or the industry leaders. Analyse their social media presence - the platforms they use, their engagement rates, the type of posts that do well. This benchmarking process not only gives an insight into what works in your industry but also helps find gaps that you may fill or new platforms you may test.

To conclude, the process of selecting your ideal social media platforms is an immersive exercise that requires conducting research, assessing your brand personality and resources, setting clear objectives, and keeping a close eye on the activities of your competitors. There isn't a one-size-fits-all answer; it's all about figuring out what fits your needs, capabilities, and objectives the best. Try, test, iterate, and evolve until you find your sweet spot.

Chapter 4. Creating a Winning Social Media Strategy

Creating an effective social media strategy is akin to developing a blueprint for a grand architectural design. A social media strategy, like an architectural blueprint, will guide your approach, help you make informed decisions, and create structures that attract and engage the audience. A strategy isn't a step-by-step guide to posting content on Facebook; instead, it's a comprehensive, versatile game plan to leverage the potential of social media platforms throughout your event lifecycle.

4.1. Understanding Your Objectives

The first crucial step to creating a winning social media strategy is defining your objectives. Ask yourself: Why are you developing a social media strategy in the first place? Objectives could range from increasing event awareness, generating engagement, obtaining attendee data, to ticket sales. This stage is critical in your social media strategy as it informs every future decision you will make. When outlining your objectives, keep them SMART (Specific, Measurable, Achievable, Relevant, Time-bound) to maintain focus and increase the odds of success.

4.2. Identifying Your Audience

Knowing your audience is half the battle. The second critical component is identifying who your audience is and understanding their digital behavior. Consider their demographics, interests, behaviors, and their preferred social media platform. Dive deep into the statistics and analytics to know your buyer-persona better. Once you have a profile of your ideal audience, it becomes easier to create content, ads, and campaigns that appeal to them and meet your objectives.

4.3. Choosing the Right Social Media Platform(s)

Not all social media platforms are created equal. Each one has a unique audience and different rules of engagement. Therefore, knowing which platform(s) to focus your energy on depends primarily on your defined objectives and identified audience. If your event targets business professionals and executives, LinkedIn may be a preferable choice. Instagram and Snapchat are platforms where younger audiences tend to congregate. Facebook offers a comprehensive blend of demographics and a robust platform for events. Twitter, meanwhile, excels in real-time news and conversation sharing. However, merely having a presence on these platforms isn't sufficient. Consistency, quality content, and meaningful interactions are crucial to achieve success.

4.4. Developing Your Brand's Voice and Tone

Defining your brand's voice and tone is an essential consideration in your social media strategy. Your voice is your brand's personality as perceived by your audience, and tone is how that personality is expressed within different contexts. Your brand's voice should remain consistent across all platforms, while your tone may vary depending on the platform and mood of the message. Keep your voice authentic, aligned with your brand's character, and ensure it resonates well with your audience.

4.5. Constructing a Content Calendar

The key to a dynamic and proactive social media strategy is a well-planned content calendar. Organize which content will be shared, when, and on what platform. Detail it out to include the caption, hashtags, and media type (image, video, GIF, etc.). It will facilitate systemizing your posts, prevent last-minute scrambling for content, and ensure a balanced mix of content types and subjects.

4.6. Utilizing Social Media Advertising

Social media platforms offer advertising opportunities with advanced targeting options, making them indispensable in your strategy. Create targeted advertisements based on your defined audience profile. Include a strong call-to-action, use compelling visuals, and carry out A/B testing to improve effectiveness.

4.7. Tracking, Analyzing, and Adapting

Finally, establishing a well-thought-out social media strategy doesn't end at planning and execution. Regularly track and analyze your progress against your set objectives using inbuilt analytics tools on the respective social media platforms. Integrate these insights back into your strategy, adapting it as necessary to ensure maximum engagement and results.

In essence, a successful social media strategy engages your audience, enhances your brand's visibility, and drives events success. It doesn't happen overnight, so stay patient, learn from analytics, be ready to innovate, and adapt to the dynamic nature of social media. This chapter provides a solid foundation for establishing your social media strategy, paving the way to social media success and ultimately, a triumphant event.

Chapter 5. Mastering Event Promotion on Social Media

Welcome to the era where events are no longer confined within the four walls of a venue; they have taken on a new dimension and broken through virtual spaces, storming the domain of social media. Mastering event promotion on this platform requires thoughtful strategies, and to facilitate easier understanding, this chapter is divided into several sub-chapters focusing on the elements of successful social media event promotion.

5.1. Understanding Your Audience

Knowing the pulse of your audience is the cornerstone of any promotional activity. If you don't know who you're targeting, how can you possibly begin to create content that appeals to them? The first step is to analyze and comprehend your audience demographics. Routinely scrutinize your social media insights, use analytics tools, and grasp a good understanding of competitor responses.

Take note of audience engagement habits - the kind of posts they interact with most, the time they're most active online, the type of language they use. This will help you to define your tone of voice, determine the type of content you create, and the timing of your posts.

5.2. Creating a Social Media Calendar

It's time to organize your promotional activities with a social media calendar. It offers a clear view of what and when you'll be sharing content. Include elements such as teaser videos, behind-the-scenes photos, live Q&As with speakers or performers, and more. With a content calendar, you're ensuring a steady stream of relevant, engaging content leading up to your event.

Scheduling your content allows you to maintain a consistent presence on social media, ensuring that your message reaches your audience consistently irrespective of time zones. There are myriad social media scheduling tools available today, make sure to leverage them.

5.3. Designing Engaging Social Media Graphics

"Show, don't tell" resonates strongly within social media spaces. An interesting image, a fascinating video, a gripping infographic - eye-catching visuals play a key role in attracting people's attention. For your event, make sure you design an eye-catching event display picture and cover photo.

Graphics tools like Canva and Adobe Spark offer extensive libraries of templates and design elements that can help you create engaging visuals, even if you're not a professional designer. Remember, cohesion between your event branding and your social media graphics is crucial.

5.4. Leveraging the Power of Hashtags

Hashtags are gateways to visibility. They improve your reach, boost post engagement, and are ideal for tracking campaign performance. Make sure you create an event-specific hashtag. Encourage attendees, speakers, and others involved in your event to use the hashtag in their posts. Their followers will see these posts, exposing your event to a wider audience.

Take the time to research popular and trending hashtags in your event's niche. Leverage these hashtags to engage with the community and improve visibility.

5.5. Using Paid Advertisements

Social media platforms offer powerful tools for targeted advertising. Facebook event advertising, Instagram sponsored posts, Twitter promoted tweets, LinkedIn sponsored ads, and more are at your disposal. Use these tools to reach a wider audience who might be interested in your event but are not currently connected with your network.

You can target your ads based on demographics, interests, online behavior, and even connections. By investing in a paid advertising strategy, you ensure that your event receives maximum targeted visibility.

5.6. Collaborating With Influencers

Building relationships with influencers can be a powerful avenue for event promotion. Collaborating with influencers, micro-influencers, or even local celebrities can give a significant boost to your event's visibility and uptake.

People tend to trust the recommendations made by influencers more than a brand's advertising. Getting influencers involved in promotion can help reach potential attendees who would have been unreachable otherwise.

5.7. Post-Event Social Media Activity

Don't let your social media stop buzzing once the event ends. Keep the conversation going. Share highlights, photos, videos, testimonials, and news of upcoming events. Be responsive to attendee feedback and comments. All of these post-event activities can help maintain the momentum gained from your event, and equate to longer term success.

We can conclude that mastering promotion on social media revolves around knowing your audience, creating engaging content, harnessing the power of hashtags, using paid advertisements, collaborating with influencers, and maintaining post-event social media activity. Putting thought and effort into these areas will go a long way toward turning your event into a successful and memorable one.

Chapter 6. Crafting Engaging Content that Rallies Audience

In the world of event planning, content is the driving force that captivates your audience, ignites their excitement, and leaves an indelible impression, long after the event has concluded. Crafting engaging content isn't a seemingly random process but a calculated endeavor nurtured with insights, understanding, and an unparalleled sense of creativity. The following discourse serves as a step-by-step guide, drenched in detail, to help you ace the art of crafting captivating content that rallies your audience and drives engagement beyond measure.

6.1. Understanding Your Audience

The creation of engaging content begins with understanding your audience. As an event planner, you need to recognize who your content is for and what will resonate with them. Begin by identifying the age range, profession, interests, preferences, and pain points of your target audience. Utilize available data, surveys, or personal interfaces to capture this information.

Next, delve into your audience's online behavior. Do they frequently engage with video content? Are they inclined towards informative blogs or are they fascinated with striking visuals and infographics? By understanding your audience's preferences, you can tailor your content to resonate with their tastes, thus enhancing its engagement quotient.

6.2. Tailoring Content According to Platform

Different social media platforms favor unique styles of content. On Instagram, visually-rich content thrives, while Twitter favors short, impactful messages. Meanwhile, LinkedIn values professional, informative content. Bearing this in mind, strategize your content creation process to align with the specific platform's norms and the way your audience interacts with the medium. This fine-tuned approach will ensure the maximum reach and engagement of your content on each platform.

6.3. Implementing Variety and Creativity

Variety is crucial in engaging your audience and preventing your content from becoming monotonous or predictable. Incorporate a mix of various content types (videos, blogs, infographics, pictures, podcasts etc.) and topics (behind-the-scenes looks, interviews, historical event recaps, future event teasers).

Creativity, too, lies at the heart of successful content. Think out-of-the-box and embrace imaginative perspectives to present familiar topics in a new light. Be playful with your words, visuals, and themes – surprise and delight your audience to keep them hooked to your content.

6.4. Focusing on Quality

Even as you strive for variety and volume, never compromise on content quality. Each piece of content published should maintain a high standard, in tone, design, relevancy, and accuracy. Investing time and effort into crafting high-quality content is a direct reflection of your commitment to your audience, which fosters trust and boosts engagement.

6.5. Incorporating Interactive Elements

Interactive content can increase engagement significantly. Q&As, polls, quizzes, contests, or challenges encourage audiences to become active participants rather than passive consumers. This active participation fosters a sense of belonging within your audience which can lead to increased attendance and lasting affinity for your events.

6.6. Telling a Story

At its core, your content should tell a compelling story that ties back to your event. Storytelling evokes emotion, fosters connection, and consequently builds engagement. Whether you're recounting past successes, presenting event highlights, or sharing attendee testimonials, weave these elements together into a captivating narrative to rally your audience.

6.7. Using Clear Call-to-Actions

Nudge your audience towards interaction through well-crafted Call to Actions (CTAs). Using imperative verbs like 'register', 'learn', 'discover', you can direct your audience to the next step, be it event registration, further content exploration, or sharing their own experiences. A successful CTA motivates quick action, propels the customer journey forward, and measurably increases engagement.

6.8. Experiment and Measure

Finally, remember that content creation is a dynamic process that requires continuous experimentation, adjustments, and enhancement to discover what truly captivates your audience. Utilize analytics to measure engagement levels and audience response. Learn from your successes and mistakes equally, and adapt your content accordingly.

By following these key guidelines and tips, you can design a foolproof content crafting strategy that heightens engagement, fosters connections, and rallies your audience effectively, ensuring not just the success of your current event, but cultivating a loyal audience for future events as well. An understanding of audience expectations, coupled with creativity and a commitment to quality, will distinguish your social media presence and equip you to harness the extraordinary benefits it can offer. Your social media platforms are a direct link to your attendees and potential attendees – captivate them with your content, and watch the magic unfold!

Chapter 7. Best Practices for Audience Interaction

Engaging with your audience isn't a one-time affair; it's a continuous process that requires constant attention and nurturing. Think of it this way, social media platforms are your digital venue, and the audience interaction taking place is your lifeblood – vital for the overall health and success of your event. So, let's delve into the successful practices that can enhance your audience interaction, turning spectators into advocates and casual browsers into committed attendees.

7.1. Strategize Your Audience Interaction

The initial step towards meaningful audience interaction lies in crafting a sound strategy. You must know who you are aiming at, what message you want to convey, and the kind of social media platforms they generally use.

1. **Know Your Audience**: Understand your audience demographics, preferences, social behavior, and their preferred social media platforms. Powerful tools such as Google Analytics, Facebook Insights, and Twitter Analytics can significantly aid in understanding your audience better.

2. **Define Interaction Goals**: Are you trying to encourage professional networking, or are you aiming to generate hype around your event? Assess your engagement metrics, i.e., likes, shares, comments, reviews, direct messages, etc.

3. **Choose the Right Platform**: Every social media behemoth serves different purposes and attracts varying audiences. Select your ideal platform(s) depending on your audience and event type.

7.2. Creating a Social Media Calendar

A well-curated social media calendar helps in planning and organizing engagement content, thereby providing consistency.

1. **Plan Ahead**: Cross the last-minute rush off your list by planning your event's social media content ahead of time. Decide in advance what content will be shared and when.

2. **Frequency of Posts**: Depending on your audience's preferences, the platform used, and the event type, decide on the frequency of your posts. Ensure that the posts are regular but not overwhelming.

3. **Seasonality and Trends**: Take note of special occasions, significant holidays, or trending topics relevant to your audience and incorporate them into your social calendar.

7.3. Personalizing Your Audience Interaction

Personalization is the key to winning hearts in today's digital landscape.

1. **Tailored Content**: Use audience insights to craft content that resonates with them. A direct, conversational tone invites interaction and also fosters a stronger relationship with your audience.

2. **Use Real-Time Data**: Leverage the power of real-time data to tailor your engagement tactics. Interact with the audience based on their current social media activities.

3. **Addressing by Names**: This deploys an old psychological trick of achieving instant connection. When you address your audience

by their names in comments or messages, it exudes warmth and personal touch.

7.4. Employing Varied Content Formats

Avoid monotony and add a dash of vibrancy to your interactions with varied content formats.

1. **Eye-Catching Images**: Images engage users more than plain-text posts. Use high-quality, relevant images in your posts to attract attention and encourage interaction.

2. **Informative Videos**: Videos are highly engaging and can explain things more efficiently than text. Live videos, behind-the-scenes, promotional trailers, or fun interaction videos can usher in high engagement.

3. **Interactive Polls, Quizzes, or Contests**: Such interactive content formats increase user-engagement, and the shared conclusions or lucky winners receive more visibility, thus pushing your event into limelight.

7.5. Responding to Audience

Timely and adequate response is as essential as creating engaging posts. Remember the 'social' in 'social media.'

1. **Prompt Responses**: Responding quickly to comments, messages, or complaints shows that you genuinely care for your audience's experiences and inquiries.

2. **Gratitude for Positive Feedback**: Don't just 'like' positive feedback. Respond with a thank you message, or even better: share it on your page.

3. **Handling Complaints or Negative Reviews**: Address the issues

straight forwardly. Ensure the audience that their issues will be dealt with promptly and sincerely.

Effective audience interaction can make a vast difference in the success of your event. By implementing the best practices illustrated above, you can cultivate a loyal and engaged audience, shine a spotlight on your events, and become a trendsetter in the digital world of event planning.`),

Chapter 8. Leveraging Social Media for Event-Day Engagement

Event-day engagement is often a gold mine that event organizers fail to exploit efficiently. Despite the rush and chaos, proper strategizing and timely engagement can play a decisive role in not just reinforcing the buzz about your event, but also catalyzing real-time marketing that could potentially expand your reach and provide immediate feedback on your current strategies.

8.1. The Power of Live-Tweeting and Instagram Stories

One of the most powerful functions of social media is its ability to document events in real-time, establishing instant connections with your followers, evoking participation and heightening their overall experience. Live-Tweeting and Instagram Stories can prove to be the game-changing tactic for your event-day social media engagement. These tools hold immense potential for creating personalized, moment-to-moment narratives of your event, thereby providing your online audience an insider's view into event happenings.

Tips and strategies for optimal usage of these functions include:

- Posting regularly: Make sure the content feed flowing is continuous and consistent. A posting cadence as frequent as every 15-20 minutes would work favorably.

- Incorporating rich media: Use videos, infographics, gifs, quotes or your event highlights to deliver a compelling story, thereby making your narratives more eye-catching and engaging.

- Live Q&A Sessions: Host live Q&A sessions on Twitter using a dedicated event hashtag. This drives interaction and answers real-time queries, enhancing the overall attendee experience.

- Showcase User Generated Content: Featuring audience's tweets or Instagram updates brings in fresh perspective and makes your followers feel more involved and appreciated.

8.2. Facebook Live And Its Influence

For bigger events, especially those involving keynote guests, high-profile panel discussions, or entertainment activities, Facebook Live provides a robust platform to live-stream the proceedings to your larger fan base who couldn't make it to the ground zero. It provides a global platform to your event happenings, thereby broadening its exposure. However, it's essential to promote your live streaming beforehand and engage viewers by responding to comments, asking for shares, or even motivating them to post user-generated content.

8.3. Harnessing LinkedIn for Professional Events

For professional, seminar or business-oriented events, LinkedIn provides a favorable platform for networking and sharing rich professional content. Extend your event-day delivery through LinkedIn's live function, create engaging posts during the event that incorporate event highlights, panel discussion key points, important quotes, and more. Share links to any live blogs or real-time resources you're creating. Also, consider having a LinkedIn photo booth at your event, where attendees can get a professional photo taken and upload it directly to their profile, thereby driving personal branding along with buzz for your event.

8.4. Snapchat Geofilters: The Fun Element

Snapchat Geofilters helps to add an extra layer of exclusivity and fun to your event. Create a unique, event-specific filter that attendees can use while attending the event. This feature not only uplifts the fun quotient of the event but, because of its shareability, it also contributes to boosting your event's visibility on social media.

8.5. Post-Event Interactions: The Icing On The Cake

Social Media activity need not halt with the end of the event. Instead, it can be used as a base to continue interactions post-event, celebrate success, thank participants, and share memorable snaps, thereby creating a warm concluding gesture. Highlight participant testimonials, share introspective posts, or teasers for your next event to keep the ball rolling.

A careful amalgamation of these strategies, blended with your event's unique flavor, will assuredly amplify your event's impact manifold and drive greater social media engagement on the day of the event itself. Remember, consistency is key and timing, priceless. Leverage the power of these tips to add a unique dimension to your event's social media coverage and garner the attention it truly deserves!

Chapter 9. Post-Event Debriefing in the Digital Age

Like a magician revealing the secrets behind his awe-inspiring tricks, we are peeling back the curtain to introduce you to an important aspect of social media management in events - Post-event debriefing in the digital age. This stage in the event-planning process is often overlooked, but it is the linchpin that reinforces your efforts, recognizes achieved objectives, identifies areas of improvement, and sets the stage for future events.

9.1. The Concept of Digital Debriefing

Let's embark on what we mean by digital debriefing. Traditionally, a debriefing refers to the practice of evaluating and reflecting on an operation, project, or event once it concludes. It usually involves discussing what went well, what didn't, and what could be improved in the future. In the digital age, this definition gets expanded. Digital debriefing drifts from physical meetings to involve gathering data, analyzing metrics from different social media platforms, analyzing audience engagement levels, evaluating feedback, and assimilating these learnings into future strategies.

9.2. The Importance of Post-Event Debriefing in the Digital Age

Digital debriefing serves as the compass that manipulates your future events' direction. By assessing your social media activity and audience interactions, you gain precious insights to gauge event success beyond just the 'turn-out' or ticket sales. Participants' engagement, event hashtag usage, content shares, comments, likes, and direct messages all become part of your post-event analysis, offering a comprehensive view of your event's digital impact, something that is increasingly integral in our hyper-connected world.

9.3. Dissecting Your Social Media Metrics

Deciphering what your social media statistics mean can often feel like cracking a Da Vinci Code of sorts. However, with some knowledge and understanding of what to look out for, this task becomes simpler.

Let's start by examining your 'reach'. This metric gives you the number of users who have been exposed to your content or event — the higher, the better. 'Impressions', on the other hand, measure the number of times your content was displayed on someone's screen, regardless if it was clicked or not. By examining these two, along with the number of 'engagements'—likes, shares, comments, retweets—you can discern whether your content stirred interest and tantalized your users to interact.

Pay special attention to 'click-through rates' (CTR) as they unveil how your call-to-actions performed. Did your audience follow the link to your event page, fill a form, or make a purchase? Uncover this with CTR.

Your 'follower growth rate' can hint at whether your event created a lasting impression that led users to want more of your content. A sudden increase during or after your event signifies success!

9.4. Comprehending Audience Feedback

Sometimes, data doesn't tell the full story. Indeed, numbers can mislead without the qualitative perspective that audience feedback introduces. Critiques, praises, and suggestions from your audience can provide a wealth of insights that would be challenging to extract otherwise.

Monitor your event hashtag for attendees sharing their experiences. Read through comments, direct messages, and emails. Are there repeated positive sentiments about specific aspects of your event? Have multiple people criticized a similar aspect? Focus on these patterns rather than isolated incidents to gather reliable feedback.

Think of this step as a digital recognition of the old tradition of listening to people's conversations after the event to know if they liked the cake or if they thought the speaker was dull.

9.5. Utilizing Feedback for Future Improvements

The ultimate goal of post-event debriefing isn't solely to pat ourselves on the back for a job well done or to wallow in the pitfalls. Instead, it's about identifying the highs and lows then leveraging them for future improvement.

Take for example, if your event hashtag didn't get much traction, you could consider advertising it more prominently in your next event. If a specific content form—like a behind-the-scenes video—garners overwhelming engagements, it tells you what your audience likes, and you can create more of such content for upcoming events.

9.6. Staying Connected Post-Event

Finally, relish in the importance of remaining connected to your audience post-event. Extend the conversation by thanking attendees for their participation, sharing highlights and memorable moments, perhaps in a montage video or a picture collage, or start the buzz for the next event. By doing so, you nurture the relationships that you've built, giving your audience reasons to stay engaged, further solidifying your social media presence in preparation for future events.

To conclude, as we maneuver in this digital age, the importance of a comprehensive, data-driven post-event debrief cannot be stressed enough. Not only does it provide measurable proof of your event's success, but it also supplies a roadmap for iterating and improving future events. After all, success in event planning doesn't come from getting it right the first time, but from continuously learning, adapting, and enhancing. So, gear up, dig into those metrics, extract valuable insights, and start preparing for your next big hit!

Chapter 10. Measuring Your Social Media Impact

The ever-changing realm of social media demands a meticulous analytical approach to quantitatively validate your social media pursuits. Measuring the impact of your social media activity is essential to understand what works, what doesn't, and how you can improve your future campaigns for better engagement and reach.

10.1. Understanding Social Media Metrics

To measure your social media impact, one must begin by understanding what social media metrics are. These are the quantifiable data points that offer a peep into the performance of your content. They help in surfacing insights that can aid your decision-making, deliberate future strategies, and gauge the success of your event promotions effort effectively. Some of the primary social media metrics include reach, engagement, clicks, likes, shares, comments, followers, video views, impressions, and conversions.

10.2. The Importance of Social Media Analytics

To descend deeper, social media analytics is where all measurement magic occurs. Harnessing these tools allows you to convert raw social media data into becoming your assets. They allow you to track, analyze and visualize your social media metrics, thereby creating a comprehensive understanding of your current social media standing. From tracking conversions to performing a competitive analysis, analytics tools can offer extensive insights.

A golden rule to bear in mind is that the choice of metrics you decide to track should be strongly aligned with your specific event's goals. For example, if brand awareness for your event is your aim, then tracking 'reach' and 'impressions' would be appropriate.

10.3. Analyzing Engagement Metrics

Engagement metrics hold great importance in defining your interaction health with your audience. They will help you understand just how well your audience is reacting to your content. Likes, shares, comments, retweets, mentions, and replies are all part of engagement metrics. A higher engagement rate indicates that your audience finds your content valuable, and they are moved to interact with it.

10.4. Tracking Reach and Impressions

Reach refers to the total number of unique users who viewed your post, while impressions refer to the total number of times your post was displayed, regardless of clicks. Tracking these two metrics can help you understand the potential audience that your content is touching. An increased reach could imply that your content resonates with your audience.

10.5. Evaluating The Click-Through Rate (CTR)

The Click-through rate (CTR) is the ratio of users who clicked on your specific link to the number who viewed your page. This metric is beneficial in determining the success of your online advertisements and the curiosity level in your audience to get involved with your event news.

10.6. Monitoring Follower Growth

Follower growth shows you how many new followers you've gained over a specific period. This measurement is fundamental to demonstrate the success of your efforts in attracting a new audience.

10.7. Measuring Conversions

Conversions are a measure of the number of users who complete a desired action, such as registering for your event, after seeing your social media post or advertisement. Tracking conversions helps you understand how effective your social media strategy is in driving actual results.

10.8. Social Media Listening

Social media listening, often known as social media monitoring, is a process of identifying and assessing what is being said about a company, individual, product, or brand on the internet. Hence, it is a vital tool in the bolsterment of your event's popularity.

10.9. Taking Stock of your Competitors

By taking the time to evaluate the social media activities of your competitors, you can gain valuable insights into what strategies work and do not work within your industry. It's a fail-proof way to avoid missteps while capitalizing on successful trends and approaches.

10.10. Utilizing Social Media Audit

A social media audit is not a scary term as it sounds, but a beneficial measure that will allow you to conduct a health check of your current social media standing. It involves taking stock of your current social media use, noting down what's working, what's failing, and what can be improved. It could be an excellent starting point to formulate your future strategies.

Measuring the impact of your social media efforts should be more than just a one-time exercise. It should be an innate part of your event planning process. Effectual comprehension of your metrics will eventually lead you to craft more rewarding strategies, thus amplifying the digital success of your events. Always remember, what gets measured, gets managed – so make sure you are measuring the right things!

Chapter 11. Staying Ahead: Anticipating Social Media Trends

Chasing and keeping up with the never-ending wave of change that is social media can seem like quite the challenge. However, with a keen sense for trends, strategic anticipation, and a toolbox of tricks to help you pivot at the drop of a hat, you'll find navigating the social media sea a breeze. Expectedly, in the dynamic environment that is social media, the ability to not just keep up, but also predict upcoming developments, can prove pivotal for your event planning success.

11.1. Identifying Emerging Trends

One of the initial steps in staying ahead in the world of social media is mastering the ability to identify emerging trends. This is easier said than done, but not impossible. It requires constant monitoring of the social media environment—reading social media blogs, being active on various platforms, joining relevant digital communities, and subscribing to industry-specific newsletters.

The key here is to be well informed and analyze the noisy data from the internet to identify patterns. A keen perspective to the shifting sands of internet culture, ability to discern the subtle signs in digital discourse and identify patterns can equip you with the ability to catch trends in their early stages.

11.2. Implementing Predictive Analytics

An understanding of predictive analytics tools is another

prerequisite to anticipating social media trends. These tools leverage machine learning and advanced statistical modeling techniques to predict future events based on historical data. By analyzing your social media metrics, they help you anticipate future trends and shifts in the social media landscape.

Such analytical capabilities allow you to understand the hidden patterns in your audience's behavior, predict their future activity, and tailor your event planning strategy accordingly. This will enable you to cater to your audience's tastes more intelligently and engage them in innovative ways before a trend becomes mainstream.

11.3. Cultivating a Culture of Experimentation and Quick Adoption

One of the most effective ways to stay ahead of social media trends is by creating a culture of experimentation and quick adoption within your event planning team. This can be done by allocating time and resources to trying out new strategies, platforms, and technologies.

Experimentation leads to innovation and learning, which are crucial for driving growth. Don't be afraid to test new waters, surprise your audience, and take risks. The faster you learn and adapt, the better you're equipped to ride the wave of change in social media.

11.4. Utilizing Influencers' Insights

In the world of social media, influencers can be seen as the modern-day oracles. They are often at the forefront of most trends, due to their deep understanding of their niche and their ability to engage followers. Establishing relationships with these influencers can be valuable in understanding and anticipating trends.

Influencers can provide insights into audience sentiment, preferences, and behaviors that might not be visible in your data. By actively engaging with influencers, you can leverage their insights for your own benefit.

11.5. Incorporating Feedback and Hosting Interactive Sessions

Hosting interactive sessions and listening to feedback can offer a wealth of information about where your audience's heads are at. An open dialogue allows you to identify the needs and desires of your audience that might translate into future trends.

For example, you could host webinars or Q&A sessions that provide platform for your audience to share their thoughts and opinions. A proactive approach to feedback and interaction will help you stay attuned to the subtle shifts in the social media mood, aiding in trend anticipation.

11.6. Observing Competitive Landscape

There's much to learn from your peers and competitors about where the social media landscape is headed. By analyzing their strategies and actions, you can extract valuable information about the current pulse of the market and gauge the upcoming trends.

Monitor their marketing campaigns, observe their interaction with the audience, and evaluate their performance metrics. If similar patterns are observed across the competitor spectrum, it could be indicative of a brewing social media trend.

In conclusion, anticipating social media trends is no easy feat. It demands continuous learning, careful observation, insightful analysis, and a bold readiness to embrace change. As an event planner in the digital age, you need to be perceptive, adaptable, and eternally curious to predict the' trends, or better yet – create your own!

www.ingramcontent.com/pod-product-compliance
Lightning Source LLC
Chambersburg PA
CBHW072220290526
45794CB00007B/2822